Holidays & Festivals Activities

Holidays & Festivals
Activities

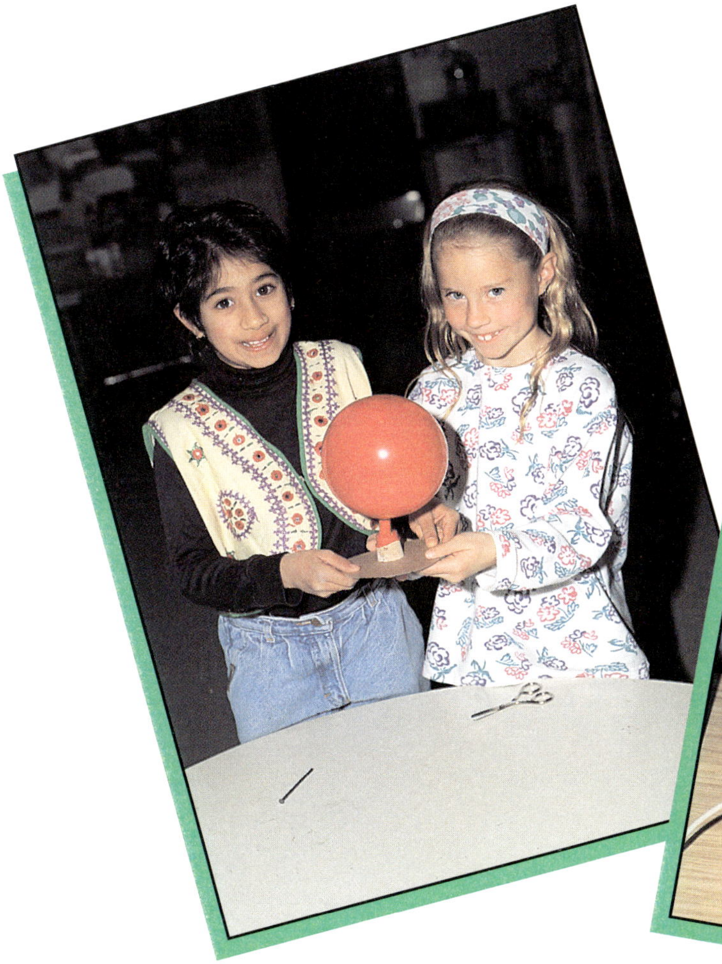

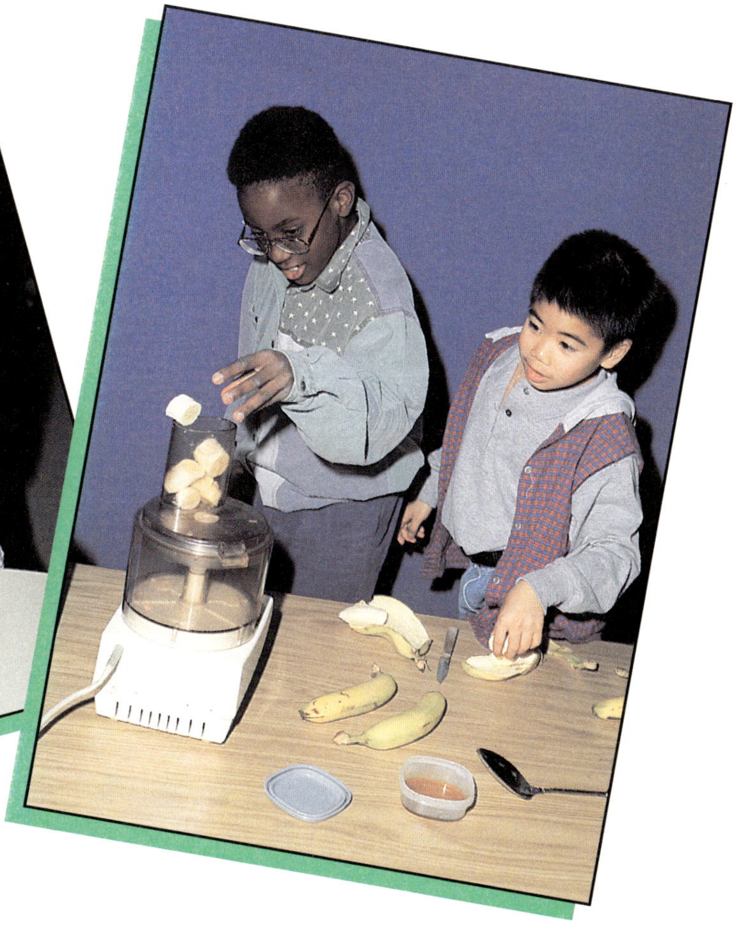

Debbie Smith

Crabtree Publishing Company

Acknowledgments

First Folio Resource Group:
Pauline Beggs — project co-ordination
Tom Dart — electronic layout/cover design
Debbie Smith — writer/editor

Design and line illustrations:
Kimberly Smith

Photographs:
Marc Crabtree

Illustrations:
Pages 6, 15 (bottom), 16, 63 by Brenda Clark
Pages 7 (top right), 40, 41, 46 by Janet Wilson
Pages 7 (bottom), 18-19, 50, 54 (bottom), 58 by Karen Harrison
Pages 8, 54 (middle) by Bernadette Lau
Page 10 by Jeff Pykerman
Pages 28-29 by Cecilia Ohm-Ericksen
Pages 32, 34, 35 by Maureen Shaughnessy
Pages 52, 53 (bottom left) by Tina Holdcroft
Page 53 (top right) by Allan and Deborah Drew-Brook-Cormack
Page 55 by Lynne Carson

Thanks to the teachers and students of St. John the Baptist School, Victoria Village Public School, and Armour Heights Public School for using the activity book in their classrooms.

Special thanks to Eric, Martin, Alexandra, and Vanessa for using the activity book at home.

Cataloging in Publication Data
Smith, Debbie, 1962–
Holidays & festivals activities
    p. cm.—(Holidays and festivals series)
Includes index.

ISBN 0-86505-121-6   Library bound
ISBN 0-86505-122-4   Paperback

This book features science, writing, and art activities for children, highlighting themes of the changing seasons, holidays, and family celebrations.

1. Creative activities and seat activities—Juvenile
literature. 2. Holidays—Juvenile literature. 3. Festivals—
Juvenile literature. (1. Handicrafts. 2. Holidays. 3. Festivals.)
I. Title. II. Title: Holidays and festivals activities.
III. Series: Holidays and festivals series.

GV1203.S59 1994   790.1   LC 94-10012

Published by Crabtree Publishing Company

350 Fifth Avenue	360 York Road, RR 4	73 Lime Walk
Suite 3308	Niagara-on-the-Lake	Headington
New York	Ontario, Canada	Oxford OX3 7AD
N.Y. 10118	L0S 1J0	United Kingdom

Table of Contents

6

Charting Changes

Changes happen everywhere, all the time. Some of these changes happen to you, such as when you outgrow your favorite pair of running shoes, when you start a new school year, or when you're finally old enough to do something that you couldn't do before. Other changes happen to your family and friends — a new baby is born, an uncle gets married, or a best friend moves away. Don't forget about the changes in the world around us! Plants grow and flowers bloom, sunny skies become cloudy, and newborn animals that wobble when they stand soon begin to romp and play.

There are many times throughout the year when we celebrate change, such as our birthdays or New Year's Day. These occasions give us a chance to think about how we and the world around us have changed and about what may happen in the future.

In "Charting Changes" you will find out about celebrations of change and other kinds of change that you may not have thought about before.

Growing UP!

Your birthday is a good time to think about how you've changed. So is the beginning of a school year.

Look at some baby pictures to see what you looked like. Now look in the mirror! What's different? Examine the color of your hair and eyes. Study the shape of your face. Look at the length of your fingers and toes. What else can you compare?

Draw a picture of what you think you will look like in ten years.

Books to read

Chin Chiang and the Dragon's Dance I. Wallace

Happy to be Me B. Kalman, S. Hughes and D. Cook-Brissenden

Ida and the Wool Smugglers S. A. Alderson

The Way I Feel ... Sometimes B. Schenk de Regniers

When I Was A Baby ...

People who have known you for a long time often have stories to tell about when you were younger. Ask your family and friends about funny things you did when you were a baby. Tape-record these stories so you can listen to them again and again, or write the funniest stories in your journal. That way you won't forget them!

I Can Do It!

What can you do now that you couldn't do last year? Maybe you can ride a bike, play a song on the piano, read a favorite book without help, or hit a home run.

Show some friends or family members what you can do, then invite them to share something that they can do.

A good way to keep track of the things you do well is to write about them in a diary or journal. Describe how it felt when you first tried something new and different. Explain how you did it. Don't forget to record the date, and draw a picture to go along with your entry.

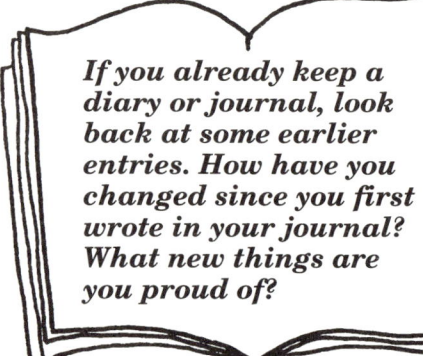

If you already keep a diary or journal, look back at some earlier entries. How have you changed since you first wrote in your journal? What new things are you proud of?

Welcome To The World!

If you have a new baby sister or brother, or if you know someone who has just had a baby, make a special present — a baby quilt. All you need are old fabric scraps in bright and cheerful colors, a needle and thread, and something to stuff your quilt with — cotton, rags, or old pantyhose.

Cut the fabric scraps into squares 6 × 6 inches (15 × 15 cm). Put two squares together, with the pattern side facing out. Place the pairs of squares side by side so you can see how big the quilt is. If you would like your quilt to be bigger, add more squares.

Think about how the different squares look together. Do they make a cheerful design? If there are squares that would look better in another place, rearrange them.

Once you're happy with your design, sew each pair of squares on three sides. Fill the squares with stuffing and sew up the last side. When all the squares are stuffed, sew them together to make a quilt.

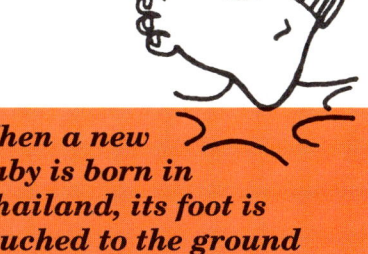

When a new baby is born in Thailand, its foot is touched to the ground three times. People believe that this will help the baby grow up healthy and strong.

In China, babies have a special celebration for their first birthday: it's called the One Year Celebration. On this day, different objects are placed in front of the baby. Family and friends watch to see which object the baby touches first. They believe that the baby's choice will tell something about its future. For example, touching a book means the baby will become a scholar. Touching a compass means the baby will love traveling.

People have made handmade quilts for hundreds of years. Many quilts have three layers: a plain sheet on the bottom, stuffing in the middle, and small scraps of colored material sewn together on the top. People help one another make quilts at get-togethers called quilting bees.

Beating Hearts

For many years hearts have been a symbol of love and friendship. That's why, on Valentine's Day, friends and family give one another cards with hearts and messages like "Be my Valentine" or "My heart beats for you."

In Wales, people used to carve wooden spoons and give them to one another as gifts on February 14. They decorated these spoons with hearts, keys, and keyholes, as if to say, "You unlock my heart!"

Your Heart

Your heart is not only for love. It helps you run, jump, and play.

Your heart pumps the blood that brings *oxygen* to all parts of your body. The blood flows through tiny tubes called *arteries*. When the heart pumps, the walls of the arteries stretch. When the heart relaxes, the artery walls squeeze together and push the blood along. For each heart beat, the artery walls stretch and contract once. This is called a *pulse beat*.

Find out how fast your heart beats by taking your *pulse*. There are several places where you can feel your pulse. One is on the inside of your wrist, near your thumb. Another place is on the side of your throat, just under your chin.

Sit very still. Place your index and middle finger on your wrist or throat. Wait until you feel a throbbing beat. To see how many times your heart beats in a minute, count the number of pulses you feel in 30 seconds and multiply by two. Ask a friend to time you.

Exercise Your Heart

Your heart rate changes when you exercise. Try some of these activities. Take your pulse after each one. Make sure you rest before each activity so your heart rate returns to normal.

- Jog in one spot for 3 minutes. Lift your knees as high as you can.

- Jump or run up and down the stairs for 2 minutes.

- Hop across the room holding one leg in front of you. Try this activity for 1 minute.

- Do 40 jumping jacks. Swing your arms above your head as you jump.

Make a heart-shaped book. On each page draw a picture of the activity and record your heart rate. Which activity made your heart beat the fastest?

How to Make a Heart-shaped Book

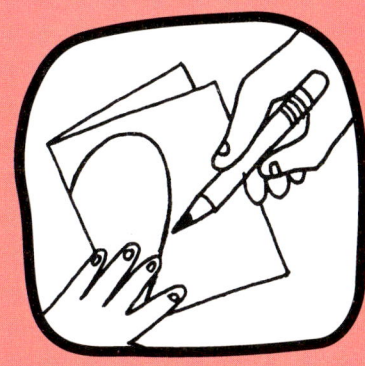

1. Fold a paper in half. Start at the folded edge and draw one half of a heart. Cut along your line. Open the paper. Use this heart as a pattern.

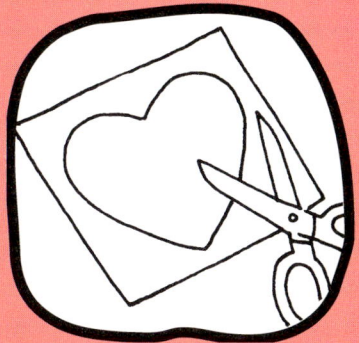

2. Trace your pattern on several sheets of colored paper. Cut out the hearts.

3. Punch a hole in the top-left corner of the hearts. Tie a colorful ribbon or string through the holes.

Holidays And Breads

The festival of Harvest Home has been celebrated in England for hundreds of years. To mark the end of the grain harvest, people bake a special bread using the newly cut wheat. This bread is placed on the altar of the church, and fruits and vegetables are displayed everywhere.

Long ago, in Scotland, friends and neighbors visited one another after midnight on New Year's Eve. They brought each other bread, cheese, and buns as signs of friendship.

Higher And Higher!

Just like the hot cross buns that people eat at Easter, many of the breads you eat are made with yeast.

Yeast is a plant that bakers put into dough to make it rise. Like all plants, yeast needs food, water, and warmth to grow. To see how yeast works, mix 1 package of active dry yeast with 1/2 cup (125 mL) of very warm water and 2 tsp (10 mL) of sugar. Watch the yeast for 10 minutes, and note the changes. Draw pictures of what you see.

After about 1 minute, bubbles form in the mixture. Soon after, the surface becomes foamy. The yeast is feeding on the sugar. As the yeast feeds it makes bubbles of *carbon dioxide gas*.

The same thing happens with dough. When yeast is mixed with flour and water, the yeast feeds on the flour and makes gas bubbles. These bubbles cause the dough to rise.

Dough Decorations

You need:

1 package dry yeast
1 1/2 cups (375 mL)
   very warm water
1 egg
1/4 cup (60 mL) honey

1/4 cup (60 mL)
   shortening
1 tsp (5 mL) salt
5 cups (1.25 L) flour
glue
water

Holiday Jewelry

Turn your holiday decoration into a necklace or a brooch. For a necklace, make a medium-size hole near the top of your decoration before you bake it. After the decoration is baked, thread a piece of string or yarn through the hole. For a brooch, bake your decoration, then attach a safety pin to the back with glue.

Sprinkle the yeast into the water. Stir until the yeast is dissolved.

Mix in the egg, honey, shortening, and salt.

Stir in the flour a little at a time until you have a ball of dough that's not sticky.

Knead the dough on waxed paper for 5 minutes.

On a cookie sheet, shape the dough into holiday decorations.

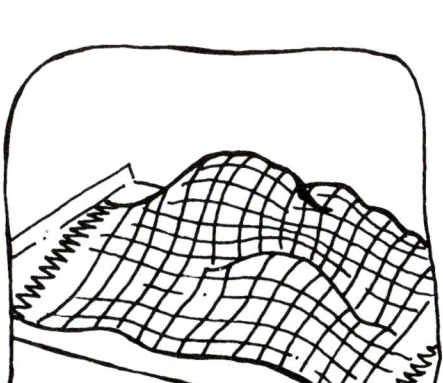

Cover the decorations with a towel and set them in a warm spot for 25 minutes. What happens?

Ask an adult to help you bake your decorations. Place them in an oven at 350°F (175°C) for about 20 minutes or until golden brown.

Mix a little glue and water together. Brush this mixture over your decorations to give them a hard, shiny finish.

Look Up In The Sky!

Sukkoth is a nine-day Jewish festival that celebrates the harvest. On the eighth day, called Shemini Atzereth, people pray for rain so that crops will grow well in the coming year.

In Sapporo, Japan, people hold a huge winter festival on the first day of February. It is called Yuki Matsuri. Skilled workers create magnificent snow and ice sculptures, and people enjoy skiing and skating contests.

Watching Clouds

One way of knowing whether it is going to rain or snow is by looking up at the clouds.

Stratus clouds look like huge pancakes or smooth sheets. When you see them, watch out! They usually bring rain or snow.

Cumulus clouds are big and fluffy. They sometimes look like cotton candy. When they turn dark, it's a sure sign of thunderstorms or snow.

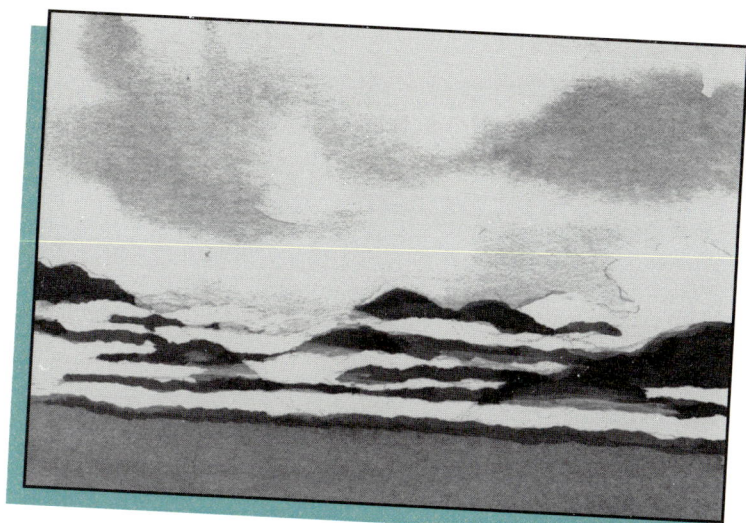

Cirrus clouds are wispy clouds that are high up in the air. They are made of ice crystals.

Weather Poems

Look up at the sky. Are clouds slowly moving in? Is thunder sounding in the distance? Read this shape poem about clouds.

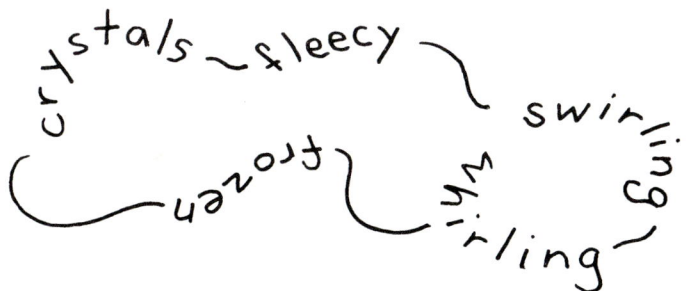

crystals ~ fleecy ~ swirling ~ whirling ~ frozen

Write a shape poem about the changing weather. Here are some words to get you started.

boomers	rumble	droplets
breezy	swirling	fleecy
glistening	sparkle	glitter
crash	shimmer	flash

Not only do people watch clouds to see if the weather is going to change, they also watch how animals behave.

Here are rhymes that describe what they see.

"When sheep gather in a huddle, Tomorrow we'll have a puddle."

"When the cow scratches her ear, It means a shower is near."

"When you see a beaver carrying sticks in its mouth, It will be a hard winter. You'd better go south."

Measure The Weather

Have you ever wondered how much rain or snow falls during a storm? You can make a weather gauge to find out. All you need is a clear container with a flat bottom, a ruler, and some sticky tape.

Place the end of the ruler even with where the rain or snow will start to collect in the container. Tape the ruler to the outside of the container.

Leave your weather gauge outside on an even surface.

When the sky clears, check your gauge to see how much rain or snow has fallen.

You can also measure the contents of the container by pouring or scooping the rain or snow into a measuring cup. How much rain or snow did you collect?

Rain Cubes

Have you ever wondered how long it takes for rain water to freeze? Here's a way to find out.

Take the rain water you collected and put it in an ice cube tray. Place your ice cube tray in the freezer and examine it every 15 minutes. Write down how long it takes the rain water to freeze hard.

As you watch, you will notice that the edges of the liquid freeze first. Then, a thin layer of ice forms on top. Finally, the middle part of the liquid freezes.

You can find out whether rain water freezes faster or slower than tap water. Fill an ice cube tray with tap water. Put this tray in the freezer at the same time as you put in the water from your gauge. Check both trays at the same time to see which freezes into ice first.

Ice Painting

You can paint with your rain cubes! First, put different colors of powdered tempera paint into shakers. Then, rub your ice cubes across shiny freezer or finger painting paper to make an invisible design. Quickly sprinkle paint on the paper, and watch your design appear.

 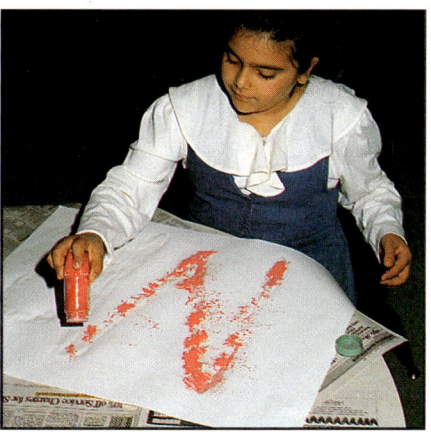

Books to read

Cloudy With a Chance of Meatballs   J. Barrett

Listen to the Rain
  B. Martin and
  J. Archambault

Time and the Seasons
  B. Kalman

Weather Forecasting
  G. Gibbons

The largest snowflake ever measured was 15 inches (38 cm) across.

The most intense rainfall took place in Unionville, Maryland on July 4, 1956, when 1.23 inches (31 mm) of rain fell in 1 minute!

There are thick yellowish-green clouds over Venus, but rain never lands on the planet. The air over Venus is so hot that the rain, which is made of sulfuric acid, evaporates before it reaches the ground.

Rain clouds look dark because they are filled with ice crystals, cloud droplets, or rain droplets that block the sunlight.

Special People

Think about all the people who are important to you — your family, your friends, your neighbors. These people may be different from one another, and they may be different from you, but they are all special to you.

Other people may be special to you even if you've never met them. You might admire the talent of a writer or the bravery of someone who has stood up for his or her beliefs and made a difference.

There are many holidays throughout the year that honor these people: Mother's Day, Father's Day, and Martin Luther King Day are just a few. In "Special People" you will find out about some holidays that celebrate important people. You will also find out about ways you can show your friends and family how much they mean to you.

Read about special people in these books from Bobbie Kalman's Holidays & Festivals series

We Celebrate Christmas
We Celebrate Easter
We Celebrate Family Days
We Celebrate Hanukkah
We Celebrate Valentine's Day

Family Days

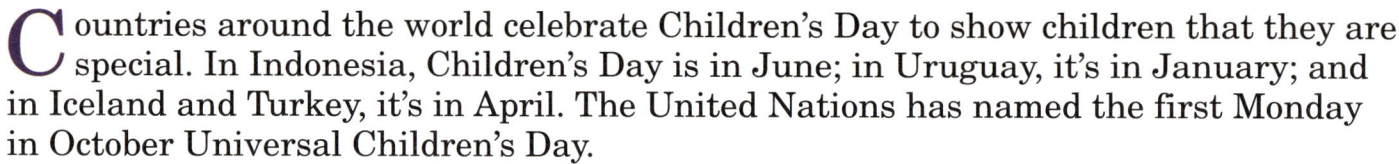

On the third Sunday in June, people celebrate Father's Day in different ways. Some families get together for a barbecue; other families do work around the house that their fathers usually do. In Wynard, Saskatchewan, children take their fathers to the World Championship Chicken Chariot Races where chickens run down a 15-yard (15-metre) track with small chariots attached to their tails.

Countries around the world celebrate Children's Day to show children that they are special. In Indonesia, Children's Day is in June; in Uruguay, it's in January; and in Iceland and Turkey, it's in April. The United Nations has named the first Monday in October Universal Children's Day.

Imagine what you would do if you had a day just for you. Write out your "wish list" and share it with your family or friends. Some of your wishes may come true on Universal Children's Day.

Your Family

Who are the people in your family? What is special about each of them?

Make a family photo album, with a page for each person. You could use real photographs, or you might draw pictures instead. Include a caption on each page that tells what is special about your family member.

If you have a tape recorder, you could record a short story about each family member. Make sure the stories are in the same order as the pictures in the photo album. As you tape the stories, ring a bell or clap your hands to tell your listeners when it's time to turn the page.

Grandma Ellen caught the biggest trout anyone had ever seen.

Avi makes hand-made teddy bears. He gave me one for my birthday.

Brothers And Sisters

Raksha Bandhan is a Hindu celebration for brothers and sisters. On this day, sisters make bracelets for their brothers using colored threads, ribbons, or glittering paper. When a sister ties a bracelet around her brother's wrist, she also gives him a candy or something sweet to eat. The brothers give their sisters a present in return. These presents and bracelets show the love between brothers and sisters.

Family Bracelets

Make a bracelet for a family member. You will need white glue, string, large pasta, and magic markers or crayons.

Measure a piece of string long enough to fit around your family member's wrist. Add an extra 4 inches (10 cm) so you can tie the bracelet.

Dip the ends of the string into the glue and let them dry. The string will be easier to thread through the pasta.

Color some of the pasta. On other pieces, write the letters of the person's name.

Thread the pasta on to the string and tie the bracelet.

Write a special note to accompany your gift.

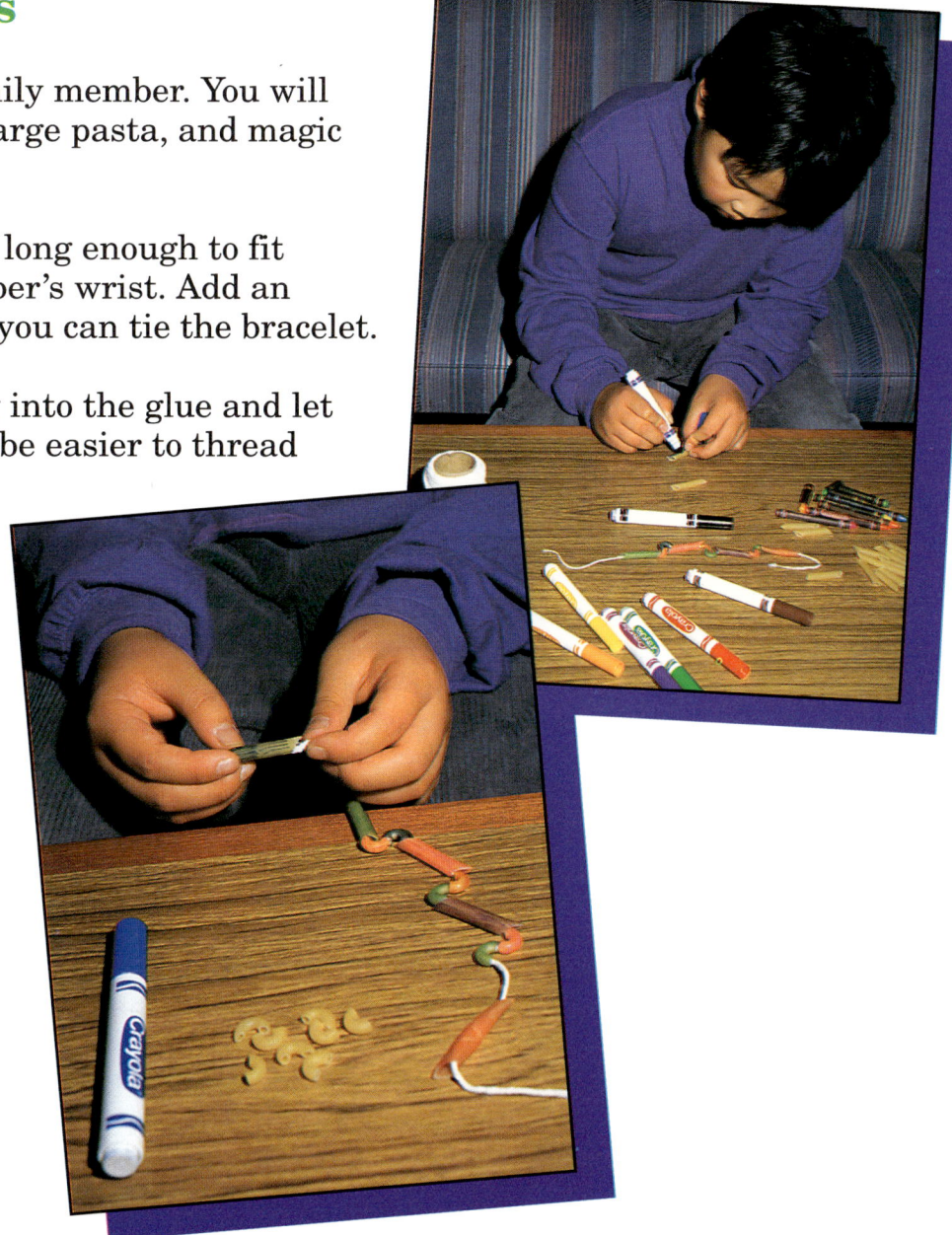

My Name Is ...

Have you ever wondered where your name comes from? It might be the same as your mother or father's, or it could be the name of another relative. Maybe your parents named you after someone in a book they read, or after a person they admired. Some names even come from other words. For example, the name Marguerite comes from the Greek word for "pearl" and the name Thomas comes from the Aramaic word for "twin."

Sometimes Christian parents name their children after saints. Saints are people who are honored because of their good deeds. Each saint has a special day on which he or she is remembered.

Find out more about your name and think of a special way to show its meaning.

Up And Down Poems

Create a poem using the letters of your name. Write each letter on a separate line — one below the other. Then, think of a word for each letter that describes you. Write it down. This type of poem is called an *acrostic*.

Name Games

What's My Name?
Choose a person's name and count the letters in it. Draw a line for each letter on paper or on the chalkboard. Ask someone to guess the name by filling in the missing letters. Print the letters where they belong, keeping track of the incorrect letters so that the player doesn't guess them again. How many turns does it take before the player guesses the name?

Smart
Unusual
Zany
Athletic
Nervous
Noisy
Energetic

Catch a Name

Everyone stands in a circle, with one person holding a ball. That person is the caller. The caller chooses a letter and says "I'm throwing the ball to someone whose name has an 'e' in it." The players then toss the ball to people in the circle who have that letter in their names. When there are no more people in the circle with that letter in their name, the person holding the ball chooses another letter, and the game continues.

Fingerprints

Just as your name is special and unique, so are your fingerprints. Each person has his or her own set of fingerprints — no two are exactly alike. That's why fingerprints can be used to identify people.

To see what your fingerprints look like, press the pads of your fingers, one at a time, on an ink pad. Then, press your inky fingers on a sheet of paper.

There are three basic patterns of fingerprints. Which of these patterns is most like yours?

| arch | loop | whorl |

Use your fingerprints to make funny-looking creatures, or to make interesting designs on note paper. Give your one-of-a-kind present to someone special.

Knock, knock.
Who's there?
Myra.
Myra who?
Myra frigerator needs defrosting.

Knock, knock.
Who's there?
Amos.
Amos who?
Amos quito bit me.

Knock, knock.
Who's there?
Sarah.
Sarah who?
Sarah doctor in the house?

Knock, knock.
Who's there?
Mikey.
Mikey who?
Mikey's stuck in the lock and I can't get it out.

Knock, knock.
Who's there?
Isabel.
Isabel who?
Isabel ringing?

Make up some "knock, knock" jokes using people's names.

Friendship

Who do you laugh with when you're happy, jump up and down with when you're excited, or cry with when you're upset? Your friends — that's who!

Friends can be young or old, short or tall. They can have loud, roaring laughs or quiet voices that sound like music.

Friendly Clues

Write clues about a friend, and put them together in a riddle. Have other people guess who the clues are about.

Here are some ideas:
My friend is 12 soup cans tall.
My friend's name has more than 6 letters.
My friend's favorite food is spaghetti.

Books to read

Amos & Boris W. Steig

Charlotte's Web E. B. White

Georgia Music H. Griffith

The Giving Tree
  S. Silverstein

A Special Trade S. Wittman

A Friendship Book

Make a present for one of your special friends.

You need:
10 × 10 inches (25 × 25 cm) fabric pieces (old bed sheets
or pillow cases)
scissors
markers
fabric crayons
hole punch
ribbon
paper
pencil

Think about what friendship means to you. Start each idea with "Friendship is … ." For example, you might write "Friendship is sharing happy times." Draw a sketch for each idea.

Choose the ideas that you like best. With markers or crayons copy each idea onto a piece of fabric. Use a pale color of fabric so your drawings and writing show up easily.

Arrange the pages in order. Make a cover for your book with the title "Friendship is … ." Punch 2 holes on the left side of each page. Make sure the holes are on the same spot on each page. Put the pages together and tie a ribbon through the holes.

Happy Birthday!

Many stories that were written a long time ago are still favorites today. The authors of these stories wrote about funny and adventurous characters who lived in beautiful and sometimes mysterious settings. Their stories make us laugh, cry, and dream of other worlds. Which authors do you think will still be favorites 50 years from now?

"Winnie the Pooh"
A. A. Milne
January 18

"The Tale of Peter Rabbit"
Beatrix Potter
July 28

"The Princess and the Pea"
Hans Christian Andersen
April 2

"Alice's Adventures in Wonderland"
Lewis Carroll
January 27

"Charlotte's Web"
E. B. White
July 11

Favorite Authors

Choose a story by a favorite author. Read the story to a friend, or tell about the story using a movie box.

To make a movie box, fold a long strip of narrow paper into sections. In each section, draw a picture of a different scene from the story.

Cut a window on one side of a shoebox. Make it the same size and height as one of your sections.

Poke two holes near the front of the lid. The holes should be just large enough for pencils to fit through.

Tape both ends of the movie strip to the pencils. Roll your story around one pencil.

Turn the pencils as you tell the story.

Story Characters

With a partner, choose two story characters to role-play. For example, you could be Winnie the Pooh while your partner might be Alice in Wonderland. Role-play a conversation between the two characters. Then, have the audience guess who the characters are.

Celebrating Light

In ancient times, people worried that the sun would not come back after the long months of winter. They needed the sun for energy and warmth. Plants needed the sun to grow and produce food. So, the people held festivals where they lit huge bonfires and asked the sun to return safely in the summer.

Many celebrations use lights as symbols of peace, hope, love, and luck. At Christmas, people string colored lights on Christmas trees and use candles to remind them of the star that shone over Bethlehem. People celebrate the miracle of Hanukkah by lighting a *menorah*, which holds nine candles. For Kwanzaa, a celebration of African-American heritage, families light the candles of the *kinara* as a symbol of their beliefs.

In "Celebrating Light" you will find out about holidays that celebrate light, and about the importance of light to both people and nature.

Who Needs Light?

Many years ago, when the dark days of winter began, people held festivals of fire and light. They were trying to strengthen the sun.

Hundreds of years ago, Celtic farmers in Europe knew how important sunshine was for their crops. Each year, on October 31, they held a fiery festival to ask for the sun's safe return. They lit huge bonfires on the hillside. When the fires were almost out, they took pieces of glowing wood to light new fires. They believed that the new fires would bring good luck.

A Plant Maze

Humans aren't the only ones who need light. Plants need light, too. This experiment shows what happens when plants get only a small amount of light.

You need:
bean seeds
soil
flower pot
box with lid and divider
scissors
water

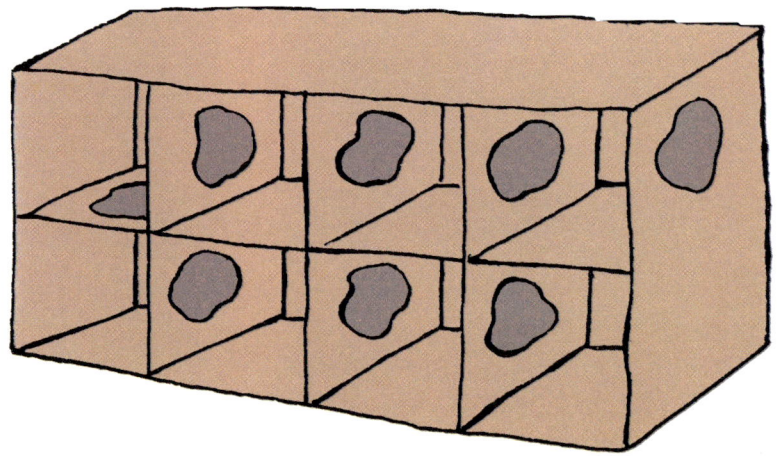

Start at one corner of the divider and cut holes to make a maze. Make the holes at least 2.5 inches (5 cm) in diameter. At the farthest corner of the box, cut a hole that leads to the outside.

Plant bean seeds in the flower pot. Place the pot in the corner of the box farthest from the outside hole.

Cover your box so that sunlight enters only from the outside hole. Every two or three days, open your box to water your plant, then close the lid again. What do you notice about your plant after 1 week? 2 weeks?

Your plant will grow through the holes of the maze, trying to find the light that enters from the outside hole.

Sun Days

Solstice is the Latin word for "the sun stands still." The summer solstice (June 20, 21, or 22) is the day when people living north of the equator get the most hours of sunlight. They get the fewest hours of sunlight during the winter solstice (December 21 or 22). It's the opposite for people living in the southern half of the world!

People celebrate the solstice in many different ways. For the summer solstice, people in Falmouth, Nova Scotia hold a huge teddy bear picnic where they give prizes for the oldest and most-loved bear. For the winter solstice, people in Victoria, British Columbia celebrate with a "Bring back the light" party. They decorate a Christmas tree, eat a potluck supper, dance to folk music, sing carols, and shout "The days are getting longer!" as each person holds a candle.

In Tuktoyaktuk, in the Arctic, the sun doesn't rise for about 3 weeks before and after the winter solstice. Around the time of the summer solstice, the sun never sets. This is why the area above the Arctic Circle is known as the Land of the Midnight Sun.

Equinox is the Latin word for "equal night." There are 2 days in the year when there is the same amount of light and darkness — 12 hours each. The spring equinox is on March 20 or 21, and the autumn equinox is on September 22 or 23.

Me And My Shadow

On a bright sunny day you notice something behind you. You turn around, and it turns around with you. You take a step forward, and it takes a step forward. What is it? It's your shadow.

Shadows are caused when objects block light. You cast a shadow on a sunny day because you block the light that would otherwise hit the ground.

Ask a friend or family member to help you measure your shadow at different times of the day. You could measure it every hour, or first thing in the morning, around noon, and late in the afternoon.

Record the size of your shadow and the time when you took these measurements. What do you notice?

Measure your shadow in different ways. Use a ruler or tape measure to measure its length. Find its perimeter by using a string to outline your shadow, then measure the length of the string.

Your shadow will be largest when the sun is lowest in the sky: that's early in the morning and late in the afternoon. Your shadow will be smallest in the middle of the day, when the sun is at its highest point.

The Star Festival

ook up at the sky on a clear, dark night. What do you see? You might spot the lights of soaring planes, the sliver of a moon, or the two stars Altair and Vega. Altair and Vega are also known as the Herdsboy and the Weaver Princess, or Kengyu and Shokujo. They are part of the legend of the Japanese holiday Tanabata.

Spotting Constellations

A constellation is a group of stars that makes a pattern in the sky. Altair is the brightest star in the constellation Aquila. Vega is the brightest star in the constellation Lyra.

What constellations do you see in the night sky? Make notes or draw pictures. Visit the library to find books that will help you name the constellations.

Hand-Made Constellations

Create glittering constellations using grid paper, black construction paper, a sharpened pencil, and a flashlight.

On a sheet of grid paper draw a constellation. Use the squares on the paper to help you position the stars.

Place a sheet of black construction paper behind the grid paper. Use a pencil to poke a large hole for each star.

Hold the construction paper so that it faces the ceiling. Turn off the lights, and shine a flashlight on the paper. The light shines through the holes of the paper, and a sparkling constellation appears on the ceiling.

Legends about stars
Star Boy P. Goble
The Star Maiden
  B. Esbensen
*Star Mother's Youngest
  Child* L. Moeri
They Dance in the Sky
  J. Monroe and
  R. Williamson

The Colors Of Light

Sunlight is a combination of different colors of light: red, orange, yellow, green, blue, and violet. Normally it's hard to see the separate colors of sunlight, but when sunlight passes through water such as a raindrop, the light rays bend. The colors split apart so that you can see each one. When the sun shines during a rain shower, these colors make a rainbow in the sky.

Try one of these ways to make your own rainbow.

Place a shallow pan of water in the sun opposite a white sheet of paper taped to a wall. Put a pocket mirror at one end of the pan. Tilt the mirror so that it reflects the sunlight onto the paper. Do you see a rainbow?

Late in the afternoon, stand outside with your back to the sun. Hold a garden hose at eye level, and spray water in an arch in front of you. With a little practice, you will see the colors of the rainbow.

Prisms

You can use a prism to see the colors of light. When light passes through the prism, it bends the light just like water does.

Experiment with prisms and light.

You need:
cardboard	scissors
flashlight	white paper
prism	a dark room

Place a prism on a table or on the floor. Behind it, hold a piece of cardboard with a small hole in the center. In a dark room, shine a beam of light through the hole so it hits the prism.

Ask a friend to hold white paper in front of the prism. Your friend may need to move the paper until the colors of light appear on it.

Crackle, Flash, Bang!

In the United States, on the Fourth of July, fireworks boom through the sky and colors burst in the air. In Canada, there are fireworks displays on July 1, Canada Day.

On the day of the Dragon Dance in the Chinese New Year, people shout, beat drums, and light firecrackers. They are trying to scare away the old year.

In the Dominican Republic, Christmas Eve is a time for parties at the beach and colorful flowers. The skies are filled with fireworks as each family sets off its own display after dinner.

The Colors Of Fireworks

Reds, blues, oranges, golds, whites. Fireworks burst through the sky in a rainbow of colors. What do these colors remind you of? Write a poem that describes what you see as you watch fireworks. Use crayons, markers, or pencil crayons in the colors you describe in your poem.

Here is one way of writing a poem — in a diamond shape.

Have you ever wondered how colored fireworks are made? Carbon, which is in all fireworks, is mixed with metallic salts. When the two ingredients burn they create the different colors. Red is made with calcium salts, white is made with aluminum or magnesium salts, and blue is made with copper salts.

Fireworks
Flashing, flaming
Flying through the night
Bursting, blasting
Boomers

Fireworks Paintings

You can create your own explosions of fireworks using paints, sponges, string, toothbrushes, straws, and other materials. Here are some ideas to get you started.

Dip a string into paint. Curl and twist the string on a piece of construction paper to make the patterns you see when you watch fireworks. Wait until each color dries before you add a new color.

Splatter painting is fun, but it can be messy! Cover your work area with newspaper. Dip a toothbrush in paint and rub it across a screen. The splattered paint will look like bursts of fireworks.

Dip a straw in thick tempera paint and make a starburst pattern on your paper. Use the tip of the straw to add tiny stars.

Planting and Harvesting

Think of all the food you've eaten today. How much of it comes from the crops we grow? Our bread comes from the grain of the fall harvest; our apples are picked from the shady orchard trees; our meat comes from animals that eat plants.

In countries around the world, people hold harvest festivals to give thanks for the food they eat and for the beauty of the world around them.

Thanksgiving is the harvest festival you likely know best, but there are others. Honensai celebrates the Japanese rice harvest; Crop Over is held in the Barbados when the sugar cane is cut; and in the small town of Megara, in Greece, there is a spring harvest festival to celebrate fish.

In "Planting and Harvesting" you will find out about other harvest festivals and how to grow plants and flowers. There also are ideas to help you plan your own harvest celebration.

Read about planting and harvesting in these books from Bobbie Kalman's Holidays & Festivals series
We Celebrate The Harvest
We Celebrate Spring

Planting Time

In April or May, the people of Thailand hold a special planting ceremony to ask for good crops. The minister of agriculture plows long furrows in a field and scatters blessed seeds from gold and silver baskets.

The Iroquois believe that corn, beans, and squash are important crops because they provide the protein that people need. They call these foods "the three sisters." The Iroquois honor these crops in two religious ceremonies. After the Midwinter Festival, which takes place before the January full moon, the Iroquois pray that "the three sisters" will grow. After the Green Corn Festival in September, they give thanks for these crops.

The biggest seeds come from the Coco de Mer tree, which grows on the Seychelles Islands in the Indian Ocean. The seeds are even bigger than beachballs, and they can weigh up to 50 lb (23 kg)!

Growing Herbs

Herbs are special plants whose leaves, roots, stems, or seeds add flavor to our food. We also use herbs in perfumes and medicines.

There are many herbs you can plant indoors that will grow quickly. Some of these are dill, mint, basil, oregano, and chives. For each herb, follow the planting instructions on the seed packages. Remember:

- Keep your plants in a warm sunny place — a window sill is a good spot.

- Make sure the soil is always moist.

- Harvest your plants by snipping off the parts you use. Snipping will also help the plants grow quickly.

Herb	Parts to Eat	What It Looks Like
Dill	Leaves, seeds	
Basil	Leaves	
Oregano	Leaves	
Mint	Leaves	
Chives	Leaves	
Parsley	Leaves, roots	

(What It Looks Like column contains illustrations labeled: dill, basil, oregano, mint, parsley, chives)

A Plant Puzzle

On a sheet of heavy paper or cardboard, draw or paste pictures of vegetables and herbs. You might also use pictures of fruits or other harvest crops. On the back of the paper, draw large puzzle pieces. Carefully cut the puzzle pieces and put them in an envelope. Invite a friend to put the jigsaw puzzle together. Then, with your friend play a game of scrambled letters. One person chooses a picture from the puzzle and writes its name with the letters scrambled. The other person unscrambles the letters to find out what the harvest food is.

Time To Eat!

Use fresh herbs to add flavor to a favorite recipe.

Pita Pizza

Mix together 1 cup (250 mL) tomato sauce, 1 tbsp (15 mL) chopped, fresh oregano, and 1 tbsp (15 mL) chopped fresh basil.

Spread the spiced tomato sauce over pita bread. Sprinkle with cheese and other toppings.

Bake in 425°F (220°C) oven for 10-15 minutes, or until the crust is browned and the cheese is bubbly.

Farmers have many sayings about life on the farm. Draw a picture of what these sayings mean to you.

"Corn's knee-high
By the first of July."

"If February brings drifts of snow,
There will be good summer crops to hoe."

"Onion skins very thin,
Mild winter's coming in.
Onion skins thick and tough,
Coming winter cold and rough."

Creamy Dip

Combine 1 cup (250 mL) sour cream or plain yogurt with 2 tbsp (25 mL) finely chopped green onions or chives, 2 tbsp (25 mL) chopped fresh dill, 1 tsp (5 mL) lemon juice, salt, and pepper. Cover and refrigerate for 2 hours or until chilled. Serve with chips, crackers, or fresh vegetables.

Peek-A-Boo Planter

You need:
milk carton
seeds
scissors
tape
plastic wrap
elastic band
paints and brushes

Cut along the right and left sides of a milk carton to make a "drawbridge." Leave the "drawbridge" attached at the bottom.

Open the "drawbridge" and tape plastic wrap over the opening. Close the "drawbridge" and wrap an elastic band around the carton to keep it closed.

Plant seeds in the container. After a week, remove the elastic band and lower the "drawbridge." What do you see?

When the plant fills the container, move it to a larger pot or plant it outdoors.

Celebrating The Harvest

In Italy, the harvest celebration is called Ferragosto. Ferragosto means August fair. Everyone takes the day off work for this celebration. They light fireworks, play music, and dance through the streets wearing costumes and papier-mâché masks.

Once every three years, people in Tomar, Portugal, hold a huge harvest festival called Festa dos Tabuleiros. This means Festival of Trays. For the celebration, women make giant hats covered with layers of bread and flowers to wear in a parade. Priests walk behind the women, carrying black pillows and silver crowns; a brass band comes next; and cows decorated with flowers follow the band.

A Harvest Festival

Plan a harvest festival for your school or neighborhood. Send out invitations or hang up posters to tell people about the event. Describe the event, and give the date, location, and time. Decorate the invitations and posters with pop-ups of fruits and vegetables, and write in large, colorful letters.

Look on the following pages for some ideas for your harvest festival.

Guess How Many

Fill a jar with unpopped popcorn. Ask people to guess how many kernels are in the container. At the end of the festival, the person who guesses the exact number of kernels, or who comes the closest, wins the popcorn.

Peaches And Peppers

This game is played with two teams. Give each team the name of a fruit or vegetable. The team names should start with the same sound, for example, peaches and peppers or carrots and corn. Have the two teams face one another, about 3 yards (3 m) apart. Assign each team a home base. This might be a wall or a line on the ground about 20 yards (20 m) behind where the team is standing.

Call out the name of one of the teams very slowly. The team shouldn't know whether you are calling its name until the very last moment. The players on that team turn and run to their home base before the players on the other team tag them. Players who are tagged join the other team. The game continues until all the players are on one team.

Harvest Hats

Before your harvest festival, make papier-mâché hats in the shape of different fruits and vegetables.

To make a pineapple hat, mix 1 cup (250 mL) of wallpaper paste with 10 cups (2.5 L) of warm water. Stir until you have a thin, creamy paste. Dip newspaper strips into the paste mixture. Cover a round, inflated balloon with 2 or 3 layers of overlapping strips. Smooth the surface with your hand and place the covered balloon on waxed paper to dry.

To make other fruits and vegetables, wrap the papier-mâché around objects of various sizes and shapes. You might use a bowl, a bottle, or a form made of cardboard or rolled newspapers.

When the paste is dry, pop the balloon with a pin. Add spines and leaves using wire, cardboard, construction paper, toothpicks, or any other materials you choose. Paint your pineapple.

Glue the bottom of the pineapple to a sturdy paper plate. Punch holes on both sides of the plate. Attach a string to each side of the pineapple hat to tie under your chin.

Harvest Puppets

Decorate carrots, potatoes, bananas, or other fruits and vegetables to make puppets. Add colorful thumbtacks for eyes; glue on yarn for hair; attach buttons for a smile or a frown. To hide your hand, pin cloth around the bottom of your harvest puppet.

Make a puppet theatre from an old sheet or a large box and perform a play.

Smoothies

Serve smoothies at your harvest festival refreshment stand. Choose 2 or 3 ingredients to make a nutritious fruit drink. Spoon the ingredients into a blender. Blend at medium speed for 1 minute. Pour the smoothie into a glass and drink up! If your smoothie is thick, you might need a spoon.

Some smoothie ingredients:

strawberries	blueberries	raspberries
cantaloupe	watermelon	honeydew
pineapple	oranges	grapefruit
grapes	fruit cocktail	apricots
apples	peaches	pears
bananas	ice cream	milk
sherbet	yogurt	honey

Flower Festivals

In medieval times, a lively festival was held on May 1 to welcome spring. People gathered flowers and decorated their homes and churches for May Day. They chose a King and Queen of May and danced around the Maypole.

Many countries still hold flower festivals to celebrate the arrival of spring. In Holland, the Dutch have tulip festivals. In Denmark, friends give one another bouquets of delicate white flowers called lilies of the valley. And, in Hawaii, people wear necklaces of their favorite flowers to celebrate Lei Day.

Have you ever wondered why people give one another poinsettias for Christmas? According to legend, there once lived a Mexican boy named Pablo who wanted to give a gift to Mary, the mother of Jesus. All he could find were weeds. He brought these weeds to the statue of Mary and, instantly, they turned into a beautiful flower that was the color of a flame and the shape of a star. This flower was the poinsettia.

Beautiful Blooms

Look around you. What flowers do you see? There might be a geranium blooming in your window box, tulips growing in a nearby garden, or daffodils sprinkling a neighborhood park.

Make a viewing frame to look at the flowers more closely. Cut out 4 strips of cardboard or construction paper that are 3/4 × 4 1/4 inches (2 × 11 cm). Tape the strips together in the shape of a square.

Look at flowers through the viewing frame. What colors, shapes, and patterns do you see? Gently touch the petals and smell their perfume. What makes these flowers different from other flowers you've seen?

A Gift Of Flowers

For a special occasion, make a friend or family member a floral stained-glass window.

Cut two sheets of waxed paper the same size. Tear different colors of tissue paper into small pieces. On one sheet of waxed paper, arrange the tissue paper in the shape of a flower. Place the other sheet of waxed paper on top, and cover with a clean cloth.

Ask an adult to help you press the two sheets of waxed paper together with a warm iron.

Frame your picture with strips of colored cardboard or construction paper.

Hang the flowers as a window decoration. The sunlight shining through makes a pretty stained-glass window.

Books to read

Linnea's Windowsill Garden   C. Björk

Miss Rumphius   B. Cooney

The First Tulips in Holland   P. Krasilovsky

Alison's Zinnia   A. Lobel

The Rose in My Garden   A. Lobel

A Flower Grows   K. Robbins

Just For Fun

Today, as part of many holidays and festivals, people do some things just for fun. On New Year's, they blow noisemakers as loudly as they can. On Hallowe'en, they dress up in costumes and call out "Trick or Treat!" On Saint Patrick's Day, they wear green clothes and drink green drinks. And, on April Fool's Day, some people play funny tricks on one another.

On a dreary day, or when you want to do something special for your friends or family, plan a "Just for Fun" day. The ideas in this section will help you prepare your celebration.

Read about holiday fun in these books from Bobbie Kalman's Holidays & Festivals series
We Celebrate Christmas
We Celebrate Easter
We Celebrate Family Days
We Celebrate Hallowe'en
We Celebrate The Harvest
We Celebrate New Year
We Celebrate Spring
We Celebrate Winter

Scavenger Hunt

Organize a scavenger hunt. Make a list of items to find and give each person the list. The object of the scavenger hunt is to be the first person to return with all the items. If the players can't find an item on the list, suggest that they draw a picture of it or make the object themselves.

Ideas For Your Scavenger List

A Mother's Day card
The first Mother's Day was celebrated thousands of years ago in a country called Phrygia. The holiday honored the goddess Cybele, the mother of all gods and goddesses.

A carp
A carp is a strong fish that swims upriver to lay its eggs. On Boys' Day in Japan, the skies are filled with kites that look like carps. The carp kites remind the boys to be strong throughout their lives.

A first-day cone
In Germany, when children go to school for the first time, they are given a first-day cone. This large paper cone is filled with candies and cookies.

Maple syrup
The sap used to make syrup comes from maple trees. It flows when there are cool nights followed by warm sunny days — usually when the temperature rises to 36°F (2°C) or higher during the day, after a night that has been 27°F (−3°C) or cooler.

A Christmas stocking

The tradition of hanging up Christmas stockings began in Holland. On Christmas Eve, the Dutch people placed their wooden shoes by the hearth. If they had been good the year before, they found a piece of fruit in their shoe on Christmas morning. If they had been bad, they found a lump of coal or a rotten potato.

An old pot

People in Denmark saved all their old pots, pans, and broken dishes. On New Year's Eve, they threw them at the doors of their friends' houses. It was a good sign if you had a lot of broken dishes outside your door — it meant that you had many friends.

Rice

People living in southern India eat pongal for their January rice harvest. Pongal is a combination of cooked rice, sugar, fruit, butter, and oil.

Pancake mix

For over 500 years, people in Olney, England have celebrated Pancake Tuesday with a pancake race. Runners hold frying pans with hot pancakes still cooking in them. At the word "Go!" they race off to the church, flipping their pancakes as they run.

A bird-shaped or animal-shaped mask

Junkanoo is a colorful parade held in the Bahamas on December 26 and on New Year's Eve. People spend months preparing for this parade, making crepe paper costumes, tissue paper skirts, pointed hats, and masks in the shapes of bird or animal heads.

A pumpkin

Pumpkins, brooms, and black cats are all symbols of Hallowe'en.

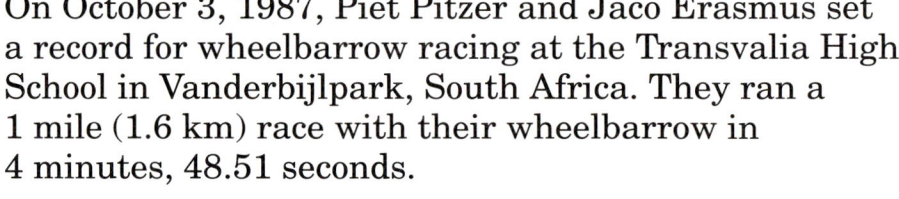

Guinness Book Record Day

Bored? Tired? Wondering what to do? Plan a Guinness Book Record Day! The Guinness Book of World Records lists all kinds of "bests" from people and nature. It answers questions such as "How big was the biggest volcano eruption?" "Who is the world's fastest roller skater?" and "What is the longest frog jump ever recorded?"

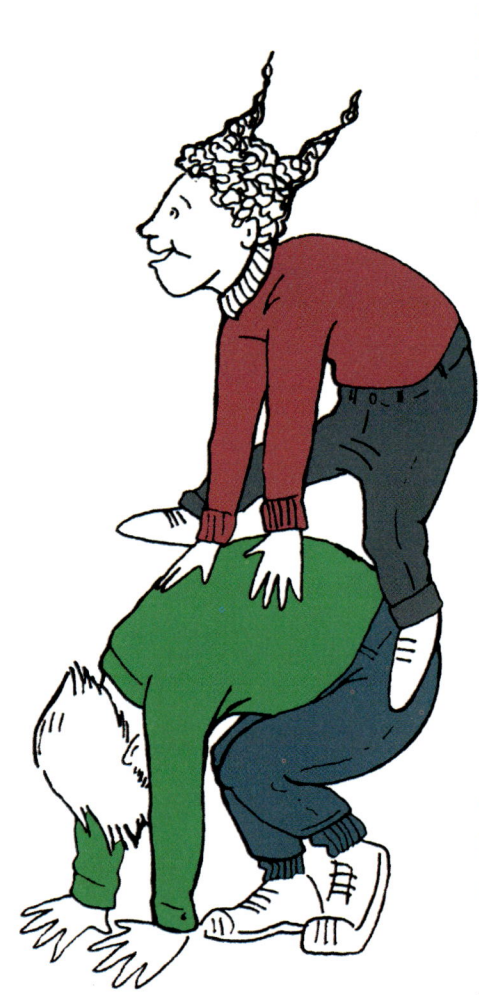

On October 3, 1987, Piet Pitzer and Jaco Erasmus set a record for wheelbarrow racing at the Transvalia High School in Vanderbijlpark, South Africa. They ran a 1 mile (1.6 km) race with their wheelbarrow in 4 minutes, 48.51 seconds.

Cathy Ushler, from Redmond, Washington, set a record for building a gum wrapper chain. Her chain was 5,967 feet (1.79 km) long and took 19 years to build.

Fourteen students from Stanford University in California set a record for leapfrogging the greatest distance. From May 16, 1991 until May 26, 1991 they leapfrogged 999.2 miles (1598.72 km). It took the students 244 hours, 43 minutes to cover this distance.

On April 23, 1990 Dale Lyons, from Great Britain, set a record for running an egg and spoon race. It took him 3 hours, 47 minutes to finish the 26 mile, 385 yard (41.95 km) marathon.

On June 6, 1988, David Stein, from New York, used a bubble wand, dishwashing liquid, and water to blow a record-breaking bubble that was 50 feet (15 metres) long.

You may wish to look through the *Guinness Book of World Record*s for ideas for your special event, or you could make up contests of your own. Give everyone plenty of time to practice and make sure that each contestant records his or her best performance.

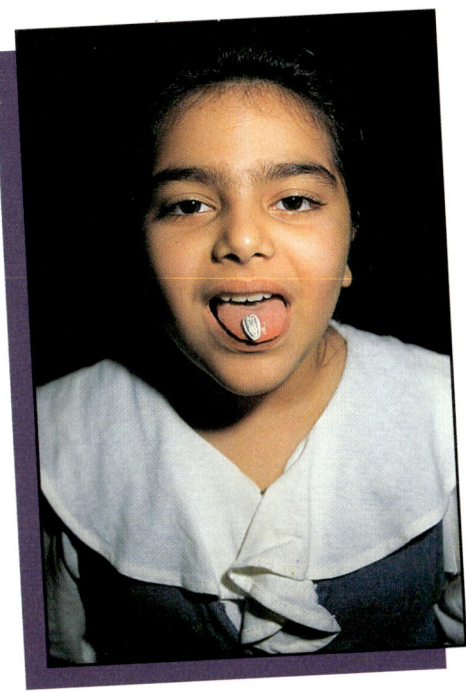

Somersaulting
Do as many somersaults in a row as you can. Count the number as you roll. Have someone be your spotter.

Seed spitting
Stand behind a starting line and spit a sunflower seed as far as you can. Measure how far your seed lands from the starting point.

Ball toss
Count how many times in 3 minutes you can toss a ball into a large container.

Building blocks
Build the highest tower you can out of building blocks. Keep track of the number of blocks you add until the tower falls.

Music Mania

Barbados holds a huge festival called Crop Over to mark the end of the sugar cane harvest. Crop Over lasts for three weeks. People dress up in fancy costumes. They have contests to choose the best bands. They also hold competitions to see who can cut sugar cane the fastest or drink the most coconut milk.

Jazz bands are swinging, crowds are dancing, parades are winding through the streets — it's Mardi Gras in New Orleans. Mardi Gras means "Fat Tuesday." This celebration comes just before Lent, the period of forty days leading up to Easter.

Imagine hearing a group of musicians playing outside your window. That's what happens in Mexico when a girl turns fifteen. Quince Anos is an important birthday for girls. It begins with a *mariachi* band playing guitars, violins, horns, and maracas. Then, there is a full day of parties, dancing, and food.

Play Along

You and some friends might like to make instruments for your own band. Use these instruments to play a piece of music, or create a rhythm pattern.

Maracas

Decorate 2 plastic bottles with paints or stickers. Put dried beans or peas into the bottles. Screw on the caps. Hold the bottles near the top and shake.

Use plastic bottles of different shapes and sizes, and fill them with different materials. Do the maracas make different sounds depending on what you use or how you shake them?

Panpipes

Use a strip of corrugated cardboard with large openings. Cut 8 straws into different lengths. Place a straw through every other opening in the cardboard so that the longest straw is at one end and the shortest straw is at the other.

To play the panpipes, blow across the tops of the straws.

String a Banjo

To make your banjo, use a piece of wood, 12 short nails, 6 elastic bands (all the same size), and paint.

Hammer 6 nails into one side of the wood. The nails should be beside one other in a straight line. Hammer the other 6 nails in a diagonal line across from the first 6 nails. You might ask an adult to help.

Paint the banjo and add designs. Stretch an elastic band around each pair of nails.

Pluck the elastic bands to make music.

Bursting Balloons

Balloons are used as decorations for many holidays and celebrations. It would be hard to imagine a New Year's party, a birthday party, or a family picnic without them!

November 13 is Pacific Balloon Day. This day marks the anniversary of the first successful crossing of the Pacific Ocean in a hot-air balloon. Ben Abruzzo, Larry Newman, Rocky Aoki, and Ron Clark made the crossing in 1981. They traveled 5,209 miles (8 383 km) in 84 hours and 31 minutes.

A Balloon Surprise

Remind your friends to dispose of their balloons in a way that doesn't harm animals or the environment.

If you're having a birthday party or another celebration you might like to give your guests a party favor. Write messages for your guests on small slips of paper. Poke each message through the opening of a deflated balloon. Blow up the balloons, and attach colorful strings to the ends. When your guests leave, offer each of them a balloon with a special message inside.

Balloon Blow-Up

You can inflate a balloon using baking soda and vinegar.

You need:
balloon
funnel
2 tbsp (30 mL) baking soda
1/4 cup (50 mL) vinegar
plastic pop bottle

Use a funnel to pour the baking soda into the pop bottle. Add the vinegar to the bottle.

Have your friend quickly stretch the mouth of the balloon over the mouth of the bottle.

Swirl the mixture of vinegar and baking soda until it stops foaming.

What happens?
When the baking soda and the vinegar mix, they produce a gas called *carbon dioxide*. The carbon dioxide fills the balloon.

See what happens when you use:
• more baking soda
• 2 tbsp (30 mL) of baking powder instead of baking soda
• a smaller bottle.

Draw a picture to show what you saw.

Bathtub Boats

Hovercrafts are vehicles that travel on a cushion of air, over water and over land. A powerful fan blows the air under the hovercraft, and propellers steer the vehicle.

You can make your own hovercraft using a balloon, cardboard, a nail, a cork, scissors, and some glue.

Cut the cardboard into a circle, about 4 inches (10 cm) in diameter. With a nail, poke a hole in the center of the circle.

Find a cork that will fit into the neck of a balloon. Make a hole through the middle of the cork using a nail and hammer. Ask an adult to help you.

Glue the cork to the cardboard so that the two holes are on top of each other.

Blow up the balloon and hold its neck closed with one hand. With the other hand, stretch the mouth of the balloon over the cork. Ask a friend to block the hole in the circle.

Set your model in the bathtub and watch it travel.

The air from the balloon passes through the hole. As the air escapes from one side of the balloon, your vehicle will travel in one direction. As the air escapes from the other side, your hovercraft will switch direction.

Index

1234567890 WP Printed in the U.S.A. 3210987